A LAYMAN'S GUIDE TO
THE
APOSTLES' CREED

H. RAY DUNNING

Beacon Hill Press of Kansas City
Kansas City, Missouri

10   9   8   7   6   5   4   3   2   1

CONTENTS

PREFACE

James B. Chapman, early leader of the Holiness Movement and influential general superintendent of the Church of the Nazarene, wrote a magnificent little booklet in which he set forth his understanding of what it means to be a Christian.[1] He suggested three essential characteristics of Christianity: It is (1) a creed to be believed, (2) a life to be lived, and (3) an experience to be enjoyed.

Christian people tend to focus on one or another of these and make it the whole of the faith. Some are strong on experience but lay minimal emphasis on ethics (living) or beliefs. There are some who make Christianity little more than a way of life, and there are some who reduce it to simply believing certain doctrines. Chapman was correct in insisting on a balance among these three elements, since the Christianity we need, as he put it, must be intellectually respectable, morally powerful, and spiritually satisfying.

He identified the "creed to be believed" as the Apostles' Creed. This early creed, he argued, is the distilled essence of the essential teachings of the Bible "so that nothing of that creed can be rejected without manifestly violating or ignoring the teachings of the Bible."[2]

While being a Christian involves more than reciting or even believing a creedal statement, everyone who wishes to have an understanding of the Christian faith should have an awareness of the basic beliefs summarized in this ancient document. As a matter of fact, sound doctrine will serve as a barrier to maverick kinds of experience that are either sub-Christian or non-Christian, even though professed under the name of Christian. As H. Orton Wiley commented, "It has been well said that this creed should be treasured in the hearts and minds of all believers and be often upon their lips."[3]

One

GOD, OUR MIGHTY CREATOR
AND FATHER

More tender than we can imagine,
    More faithful than we can conceive,
Stronger than we can envision,
    Wiser than we can believe—

What loss through our blindness we suffer
    When God's boundless love we ignore;
But when we just taste of its sweetness,
    'Tis then we fall down and adore![1]

—LAURIE H. DU BOSE

1

The Nature of Creeds

There are some who reject all creeds as being man-made and therefore not to be taken seriously. Quite often they suggest that all we need is the Bible. No Protestant would seriously question the fact that the Bible is the final authority for life and belief for the Christian. But the Bible is a complex document, obviously requiring interpretation, and the average reader probably needs considerable help in identifying the central message of this Book.

It is for that reason that followers of Christ have, from the beginning, created formulas to embody essential aspects of the Christian message in a succinct form. Even those who subscribe to the formula "No creed but Christ" are subscribing to a creed they did not derive from the Bible. Creedal affirmations are unavoidable.

Actually, scholars have clearly demonstrated that there are numerous creedal statements within the New Testament itself, testifying that, very early, Christians produced confessions to embody in a formalized way particular facets of the faith.

Since Christianity is not a system of ideas but an attitude toward a certain historical person, perhaps the earliest creed was the simple statement "Jesus is Lord." All persons who were acknowledged as followers of the Way were identified by confessing this truth. That it was not a superficial recitation is clear from Paul's words in 1 Cor. 12:3, "No one can say 'Jesus is Lord' except by the Holy Spirit" (NRSV). This implies, as British theologian Alan Richardson says, that "the acceptance of Christianity as our own personal religion is not a mere assent to an intellectual proposition, but the living response of our whole personality to the fact of Jesus."[1]

There are numerous other examples of more extended creedal statements in Scripture, as well as hymns that embody doctrinal truth. One of the most obvious is cited in 1 Tim. 3:16—"He was revealed in flesh, vindicated in spirit, seen by angels, proclaimed among Gentiles, believed in throughout the world, taken up in glory" (NRSV). These excerpts are usually identified in modern-language versions by a special literary form. Most scholars agree that the familiar words of Paul in Phil. 2:6-11 are a quotation from an early Christian hymn and are filled with doctrinal content about Jesus from His incarnation through His exaltation.

There is much confusion in the last decade of the 20th century over the issue of styles of worship. Much of the discussion revolves around the music employed in the public worship service. If the New Testament provides any clue, it would suggest that the hymns with sound theological content should be a staple of Christian worship. Of course, first-century hymns have little to do with the type of music used in contemporary churches. The believers in the first century probably chanted, and the idea of harmony did not enter as a musical form until much later. However, the content was designed to reinforce the faith, not simply become an occasion for the expression of emotion through music.

Most creeds begin with the statement "I believe." A proper understanding of these words in a Christian setting includes far more than an intellectual affirmation of the acceptance of certain facts. At least in an authentically Christian confession, it involves two things: (1) It means I am identifying myself with a community whose very existence depends upon the truths being affirmed, and (2) it means I am affirming belief in an interpretation of reality upon which I stake my whole life and destiny and that gives meaning to my personal and corporate world. Thus, it is not an individualistic statement, and it is a life-transforming belief, not merely head knowledge.

The Origin of the Creed

The specific origin of the Apostles' Creed is shrouded in mystery. An exposition of the creed written in A.D. 404 by Tyrannius Rufinus relates a legend that enjoyed much popularity for many years. According to the tale, the apostles were preparing to go forth in the power and gifts of Pentecost to preach to the nations of the world:

> As they were therefore on the point of taking leave of each other, they first settled an agreed norm for their future preaching, so that they might not find themselves, widely separated as they would be, giving out different doctrines to the people they invited to believe in Christ. So they met together in one spot and, being filled with the Holy Spirit, compiled this brief token, as I have said, of their future preaching, each making the contribution he thought fit; and they decreed that it should be handed out as standard teaching to believers.[2]

This tradition was later expanded to include the belief that each of the Twelve contributed a phrase to the creed. Such an explanation was very popular and generally accepted throughout the Middle Ages. With the rise of historical criticism, however, this legend was demonstrated to be just a legend without foundation. Scarcely anyone today would attribute the Apostles' Creed directly to the apostles.

Most scholars believe the creed was the result of a progressive enlargement of a simple ceremony of baptism, its structure clearly reflecting the Great Commission found in Matt. 28:19. The most immediate forerunner of the creed is generally recognized to be a baptismal confession used in the Christian church at Rome and known as "the Old Roman Symbol." As believers were publicly and formally inducted into the Christian faith, they were to recite the beliefs to which they were committing their lives, similar to baptismal rituals in use today in most churches.

There are two major theories concerning the purpose for such a creed, the Apostles' Creed in particular. A leading scholar of the history of Christian thought of an earlier generation, A. C. McGiffert, advanced the theory that it arose as an effort to correct the heresies propagated by a teacher named Marcion. While most contemporary scholars question this theory, some do allow for the possibility that a Marcion-like teaching was a factor in the formation of the Old Roman Symbol. At the least, it highlights the fact that much Christian doctrine was formulated in response to teachings that the Church recognized to be contrary to its major commitments. Thus the heretic makes the theologian.

The other theory about its intended function suggests that it was formulated for a catechetical purpose, that is, to teach new converts the heart of the faith they had embraced. One leading scholar points out the importance of this function in the light of the fact that so many new converts were swelling the ranks of the Early Church with no religious background from Judaism, as was true with the earliest converts. They were thus bringing their pagan ideas into the Church, and if they were not well instructed in the essentials of the faith, they could be instrumental in moving the Church away from its moorings.[3] One can readily see how this creed might serve a similar function in the contemporary Church when people without background in the Christian faith are brought into the fellowship of believers. Experience is not enough to keep the ship on course.

Furthermore, it has been suggested that the creed served an evangelistic function to give guidance to missionary preaching. This was explicit in the myth referred to by Rufinus.

Whatever its historical origin, the Christian Church has all but unanimously agreed that this is the substance of belief upon which all Christians can agree, and most Christian congregations recite, at least at times, this creed as their confession of faith.

The Structure of the Creed

Notice that the creed is divided into three "articles" corresponding to the three Persons of the Trinity. Most of the ancient creeds reflect this pattern. While the teaching about the Trinity is a great mystery that ultimately exceeds the capacity of the finite mind to fully comprehend, it is the most distinctive of Christian doctrines. It is not a problem added to other doctrines to make life difficult; neither is it logical nonsense. Rather, it reflects the Christian conviction that God has made himself known to human persons, and that this disclosure has a threefold aspect: He unveils himself as Father, as Son, and as Spirit, but these are all manifestations of one undivided God. David H. C. Read puts it in a simple but satisfying way: we experience God as always and everywhere (that's the Father), as there and then (that's the Son), and here and now (that's the Spirit).[4]

Historically, Christian thinkers have affirmed their faith that not only has the one God manifested himself in a threefold way, but He is also triune in the His essential being. The basis for this faith is the confidence that the God whose essential nature is love would not reveal himself as other than He is in himself.

Persons who insist on reducing everything to completely rational terms have traditionally had trouble with the Christian doctrine of the Trinity. The Unitarians rejected it by denying the deity of Son and Spirit; modern-day Jehovah's Witnesses reject it on the basis of what they call "common sense"; and certain contemporary Pentecostal sects deny it by teaching a unitarianism of the Son, commonly called "Jesus only." All these stand outside the boundary of historic, orthodox Christianity, which affirms as central to its belief about God that He is triune in His self-revelation.

Scholars have entered into extremely intricate and profound discussions in an attempt to provide ways of putting the Trinitarian structure into words. Since the terms they used included highly technical vocabulary derived from various philosophies of the times, an intimate knowledge of early Greek philosophy as well as the Greek and Latin languages would be essential to following their carefully argued positions. Consequently, we may merely note a few practical implications.

First, the Trinitarian nature of God guarantees that He is accessible to human experience. If He were totally remote and had not entered into our realm through the Incarnation and His Spirit, we would have no awareness of Him at all. Also, this Trinitarian nature makes possible Christian experience. Both the Son, who warrants acceptance by the Father, and the Spirit, who actualizes God's presence in human life, are essential to our relation to the Father.

It is interesting that so-called Christian movements that do not take seriously the Trinitarian nature of God do not have any vitality and eventually die. There must be some practical truth to the claim that the Trinity is essential to vital Christian experience and life.[5]

We now turn to an exposition of the creed, taking into account both the ancient teachings it clearly refutes and the meaning it may have for those of us who live in the last days of the 20th century.

ᴗ Putting This Chapter to Work

Something Conceptual: Key Ideas

A. Review the key ideas in chapter 1.
   1. The Christian life needs the balance found in the statement by J. B. Chapman. Christianity is
      "a creed to be believed"
      "a life to be lived"
      "an experience to be enjoyed" (see the preface).
   2. No one lives without a creed—even if it is not written or carefully thought out.
   3. The Christian creed is a living response to the Person, Jesus. (See the Alan Richardson quote.)
   4. Commitment to Christ is a commitment to a *community* of faith and to the Christian interpretation of reality.
   5. Christians from the earliest days used creedal statements, such as 1 Tim. 3:16; Phil. 2:6-11; and Matt. 28:19.
   6. The heresies we oppose often provoke us into making written affirmations of belief.
B. Review the preface and chapter 1.
   Mark the places where the key ideas are treated. After pondering these matters, select two of the key ideas and write in your spiritual life journal or notebook an explanation of them in words a 10-year-old can understand.

Something Devotional: Spiritual Reading

Spiritual reading is often called reading for holiness. First Tim. 3:16 is one of the early creedal statements. Read that statement several times, accenting different words. Listen to the Word with your heart. On the blank lines, write your personal response.

Great indeed, we confess, is the mystery of our religion

He [God] was manifested [revealed] in *flesh,*

---

vindicated in the Spirit
vindicated in the *Spirit*
seen by angels
preached among the nations
believed on in the world,
seen . . . preached . . . believed on

Taken up in *glory*
Taken up in glory

(Compilation of NIV, NKJV, and NRSV)

Something to Do: Table Grace

The next time you sit down for a meal with family or friends, put a copy of the Apostles' Creed at each plate. Use it as a table grace. Three different persons could read one of the paragraphs, or articles, of the creed.

Wouldn't it be great if your mealtime conversation was about the core of the Christian faith instead of television celebrities, politics, or the neighbor's noisy dog?

2

[handwritten: Who believes? I / I do what? Believe / Basis for all the rest]

One Creator with Power
and Character

[handwritten: What does it tell us about God? / What do these mean?]

The first article of the Apostles' Creed affirms briefly: "I believe in God the Father Almighty, Maker of heaven and earth." This is not a declaration against atheism. While belief in God is doubtless the most fundamental assertion of faith (see Heb. 11:6), this article is not intended to assert a theoretical belief in the existence of God as over against possible unbelief. God's existence is assumed here as it is in Scripture. No effort is made in either place to advance "proofs" for the existence of God. Such an effort occurs only when the personal reality of God has faded. Rather than existence, the most important question to the biblical person concerns the nature of the God with whom we have to do. The same is true with the creed.

Historically, the primary purpose of this first article was to declare the unity of the God of creation and the God of redemption. Certain early thinkers like Marcion (see page 12), known as gnostics, had been influenced by the assumption that matter was evil, and therefore God could not have "dirtied His hands" by creating this material world. Also, there were certain passages in the Old Testament that they found difficult to reconcile with the teaching of Jesus about God. Many people today have the same difficulty.

Marcion attempted to solve these problems by teaching that there were two Gods. Other forms of gnosticism taught that there were intermediary beings, one of whom was the "creator" or designer of this physical universe. In a word, there was an inferior deity who brought the world into being. This lesser being, according to Marcion, was the God of the Jews about whom the Old Testament speaks and who was responsible for the authorization of the slaughter and violence attributed to Him in places like the Book of Joshua. The other deity was the God and Father of Jesus Christ, the high God of whom the New Testament speaks and who seeks humanity's salvation as a God of love.

Early Christian leaders vigorously rejected this division and insisted on one God who is both Creator and Redeemer. Thus, implicitly they were holding that the Old Testament is a valid part of the Christian Bible and witnesses to the same God who manifested himself in Jesus Christ.

Many Christians today, for all practical purposes, have rejected the Old Testament by relegating it to an inferior role in their study and reading. Perhaps one reason for this is that they, like these early people, have difficulty reconciling some of the pictures of God drawn there with the picture of Him they see in the teaching of Jesus. This is a too-easy way out that the Christian Church has resisted from the beginning. What we need to do is work at discovering the proper way of interpreting the Old Testament rather than throwing it out of our Bible.[1]

Certain views of biblical inspiration simply intensify the problem. If one takes a fully literalistic or dictation theory that holds the Bible to be dictated by God, word for word, no type of interpretative device can resolve the problem. In this case we would be compelled to reject the Old Testament as unworthy of Christian faith. However, if we accept the view that God's revelation of himself occurs in the context of human understanding, we have a viable way out. In other words, God's will is received in terms of one's cultural and historical situation. This position is thoroughly consistent with a Wesleyan perspective in which God relates to human beings in a personal way and not as a typist to a typewriter. Thus, the explanation of the difficulty by Wright and Fuller relieves the problem and "gets God off the hook":

> Did God actually tell Joshua to carry on such terrible slaughter, involving even the defenseless elements of the population? It is rather difficult for a Christian to understand how God could be responsible for such a slaughter. From the biblical perspective we may perhaps frame an answer somewhat as follows: In the context of human sin, wars and conflicts occur. But God has not withdrawn from the world to heaven. He is not defeated by human sin; even this he uses for his own ends. Unless he did we would have nothing in this earth for which to hope. Yet to say that God is in control, even of our wars and cruelty, does not mean that he is responsible for the way in which men carry them on. . . . Two things must be held together in tension here: one is God's control and direction of history to his own ends, and the other is the terrible sin of man for which he is responsible. If we view the conquest in this light, then the Christian may say that God was "fighting for Israel," though his own purposes were larger than Israel understood at that moment.[2]

Perhaps the unique feature of this first article is the joining of the predicates "Almighty" and "Father" in speaking of the character of God. One speaks of ability and power; the other speaks of love, caring, and acceptance. They condition and modify each other. The God who is almighty is the Father; the Father who loves is the Almighty One. This connecting together speaks eloquently of the Christian's understanding of God. When we speak of power, we commonly think of God's omnipotence and sometimes enjoy speculating about the possibilities of that power. But the creed cautions us at this point to keep in mind that the possibilities of the Christian God are the possibilities of *love:* God can do anything love can do.

Another way to express this truth is to say that "God's power is not a characterless power." This precludes all those mind-boggling, childish questions that sometimes arise when we try to make sense of "naked power," such as "Can God bring it about that twice two equals five?" Or, "Can God create a stone so big that He can't roll it away?" As the great 20th-century theologian Karl Barth said, the power of God "is the power of His free love in Jesus Christ, activated and revealed in Him."[3]

The belief that God the Redeemer is also the Creator explicitly affirms the goodness of creation and the possibility of salvation in this life (against the gnostics). It also declares confidence in God's providential care of the world.

We have already noted the gnostic tendency to depreciate the material world, which included the body. The implication is that we can never be free from sin in this human existence, as long as we are in the body; thus salvation can only occur as an escape to a "spiritual" world. The gnostic systems developed elaborate ways of avoiding the defilement of the flesh and imagined fantastic pictures of how the soul may escape the bonds of this life to the realm beyond.

But the affirmation of the goodness of creation denies that we are bound to sin as long as we are "in the flesh." Many people even today misunderstand Paul's words in Rom. 8:8 to be saying this. They fail to note that in the very next verse he says to these fully human Romans, "But you are not in the flesh; you are in the Spirit" (NRSV). It is true, as the apostle says in verses 19-23, that the created world has suffered because of the Fall and, like the redeemed in the present, will fully be redeemed in the future. But he soon exhorts the Romans to present their *bodies* as a living sacrifice (12:1). In a word, the body can be sanctified because it is the good creation of God. As Archbishop William Temple once said, "Christianity is the most materialistic of all religions."[4] It takes the physical world seriously because God created it.

There are certain modern versions of this ancient gnosticism that this article also excludes from orthodox Christian doctrine. So-called Christian Science teaches the same fallacy about matter and seeks to maintain an independence from the pain, sickness, death, and sin that accompanies mortal existence by affirming faith in the "spiritual." As one of my former church history professors once said, they can do this only by "following the pay streak in America."

Even within the bounds of orthodox Christianity, this affirmation raises a caution against a kind of mystical spirituality that retreats into private contemplation and avoids involvement in the messy world. True spirituality manifests itself by engaging redemptively with the real world around us, not escaping from it. This is what the German theologian Dietrich Bonhoeffer called "worldly holiness."

This affirmation of faith in "the Father Almighty" is furthermore a declaration of God's watch care over His world and His people in the face of all evidence to the contrary. When evil seems to prevail, we are tempted to abandon one or the other of the divine attributes, to question either God's love or His capacity to do something about it. But to faith, since the God of creation and the God of redemption are the same, we have confidence that in love He is in charge and is working out His purposes in our lives.

In summary, we may say that this first article is fundamental to Christian faith and sets the context for life in the world lived from a Christian point of view.

❧ PUTTING THIS CHAPTER TO WORK

Something Conceptual: What Is God Like?

This chapter cites some important aspects of our God. He will always be greater than our concepts of Him. Nevertheless, He does reveal himself to us. Part of what we have learned about God is declared in the creed and described in this chapter.

Using pens, pencils, or markers of three different colors, mark up your book. Mark the best of what the author has to say about God's
> Unity (blue)
> Goodness (yellow)
> Almightiness or Omnipotence (green)

Something Devotional: **A Poem of Praise**

A cinquain is a five-line, 11-word poem.

Line 1 is a one-word title, a   *God*
  noun. In this case, *God.*

Line 2 contains two words that   _____ _____
  describe the title, God.
  Select descriptors from
  chapter 2, or use your own.

Line 3 contains three action words   _____ _____ _____
  or a phrase about God.

Line 4 describes a feeling   _____ _____ _____ _____
  about the title word
  (God) in exactly four
  words.

Line 5 contains one word that describes,   _____
  refers to, or even repeats
  line one, the title (God).

There—and you always thought you couldn't write a poem!

Something to Do: **Prayer and Witness**

1. Make the poem you wrote your daily prayer of praise for several days. Record it in your journal. Share it with friends. Witness to someone, sharing your cinquain. Explain why God means so much to you.

2. If you didn't care for your own poetry, meditate on the Du Bose stanzas on the first page of part one. Select a phrase such as "more faithful than we can conceive" or "wiser than we can believe." Prayerfully reflect on the phrase that glues itself to your heart.

Two

JESUS CHRIST OUR LORD

I say, the acknowledgment of God in Christ
Accepted by thy reason, solves for thee
All questions in the earth and out of it.[1]

—ROBERT BROWNING

He became what we are that He might make us
what He is.[2]

—ATHANASIUS

3

Who Is This Jesus?

The paragraph about Jesus Christ is the longest of the three segments of the creed, and for good reason. All Christian thought is an elaboration of the meaning of Jesus Christ. It is a spelling out of the implications of the Christ-event for both love and belief. And it further reinforces the truth that Christianity is not a system of ideas, but a commitment to a historical person. Consequently, the historical aspects of the person and work of Jesus are especially emphasized.

One reason for this is the tendency of early thinkers, under the influence of Greek thought, to deny the humanity of Jesus while holding to His deity. The tendency of most modern persons is usually in the opposite direction. We don't have as much difficulty believing that Jesus was a fully human person as we do comprehending that He was God in the flesh. But this article implicitly declares both truths without providing a theoretical explanation of either.

One of the major reasons for the reluctance to affirm Jesus' human nature in those early centuries was the influence of the gnostic premise about matter being evil, as we noted above. Consequently, here we can see how important the first article of the creed is in establishing the truth of the second. If God created the material world, it is good, and there is no real reason for questioning the possibility that God could indeed incarnate himself in bodily form.

The doctrine with which we are dealing here is technically known as the Incarnation. It is taken from the Greek word meaning "flesh" and could be roughly rendered as "en-flesh-ment." The Son of God became flesh, taking upon himself the full form of man. This is so important to Christian belief that John in his first letter stated that anyone who denied that Jesus had come in the flesh was of the spirit of antichrist (4:2-3).

The Book of Hebrews is a good resource to identify the scriptural basis for these beliefs. If one would read through the entire book, marking those verses that stress both the deity and humanity of Jesus, it would be revealing. You would find some of the most exalted passages in Scripture concerning His divine origin and nature, which at the same time speak with great eloquence about His full humanness.

This truth has tremendous practical significance. As Hebrews points out, Jesus' temptations were real because He was like us in every respect, "sin apart." Therefore, says the writer, "We do not have a high priest who is unable to sympathize with our weaknesses" (4:15). But more, He is able to give support to those who are tested. Understanding and help! Those are two benefits we derive from the Incarnation. And there are more.

The second article gives a brief summary of the entire career of Jesus of Nazareth from its conception to its completion, which has not yet occurred. One of the most important implications of this synopsis relates to the distinctive nature of the Christian faith. Unlike many other religions of the world, Christianity is not a system of ideas but is based upon certain historical events. This means that it is not a philosophy, even a philosophy of life. Rather, it affirms that God has acted in history in a redemptive and revelatory way.

One aspect of this characteristic is that it assumes a

special way of knowing. One cannot arrive at a knowledge of particular historical events through reason or reflection or meditation. Contemporary emphases on meditation in movements like the so-called New Age Movement, especially in an effort to "get in touch with oneself," are thus antithetical in principle to the Christian faith. Apart from an individual's being personally present at a historical event, knowledge of such events must be passed along by those who were eyewitnesses to those who were not. This truth highlights the importance of Scripture as the vehicle that mediates to us the accounts of the Christ-event and its meaning.

It was this aspect of Christianity that was a stumbling block to the Greeks, as Paul noted in 1 Cor. 1. The dominant Greek way of acquiring knowledge was through reason, which many believed could apprehend universal truths. History, on the other hand, was less than real and could never be the locus of eternal, universal truth. Thus, it was offensive to them to claim that the meaning and purpose of the universe could be found in a particular historical event. This is what is sometimes called the "scandal of particularity."

This "scandal" still bothers a lot of people, since they have difficulty believing that we can have knowledge of a historical event that is claimed to mediate divine revelation. While it is true that historical knowledge is not simply acquired, as the scholar knows, the Christian believes that God has somehow vouchsafed a reliable transmission of such knowledge through the Scripture. However, in common with all the other ancient creeds, the Apostles' Creed says nothing about the Bible. Belief in the Bible is not an *expressed* article of faith for the Early Church, but the belief that God's self-disclosure has occurred in historical events implies it. Actually, the Apostles' Creed probably predates the final formulation of the New Testament.[1]

What is missing from the Creed?

Bible

The second article naturally divides itself into three paragraphs, each with a different emphasis. The first speaks about who Jesus was in terms of titles ascribed to Him by the Early Church. The second briefly refers to His origin, while the third stresses what may be called "the work of Christ."

His only Son. Before examining the significance of the various titles used of the Second Person of the Godhead in the creed, we should take note of the use of the term "only." It no doubt was stated to reject the teachings of the gnostics who flourished in the second century. These systems were developed, in part, on the assumption that there was an insurmountable chasm between God and the world. This chasm was bridged by a series of intermediary beings, each lesser in being than the one above. Thus, there was a hierarchy of beings, sometimes called "angels" in Jewish circles. Each of these semidivine beings were given names and served as a mediators between God and the world of human persons.

More than one of the gnostic systems had one of these beings named "the Logos," the same Greek word translated in John 1 as "the Word." It would be fair to suggest that these many beings were seen as "sons" of God. But the Christian faith positively affirms that there was one Son *only.* Paul declares the same truth in Col. 2:9 and 1 Tim. 2:5 in the face of similar fantasies in his day.

Such fantasy systems as we can read about, for example, in the works of Irenaeus in the second century seem very foreign to our thought world. But the creedal emphasis on the uniqueness of Jesus Christ, God's *only Son,* is relevant to the need for contemporary Christians to hold firmly to the exclusiveness of Jesus Christ.

There are many who offer other revelations from

God than through Jesus. Usually one defining mark of a religious cult is its claim to go beyond the final word from God in Jesus Christ to some further "revelation" such as the Book of Mormon or *Science and Health with Key to the Scriptures*. But to add "additional" truth to that already revealed in Jesus Christ, or to claim other ways of salvation than that provided by His work, is to move oneself outside the boundary of essential Christian truth. This is why good Christian theologians insist that there can be no authentic Christian teaching that is not consistent with the revelation in Christ. He alone is the Touchstone for truth, life, and salvation.

And in Jesus Christ. Twentieth-century Christians have become so accustomed to *Jesus Christ* as a proper name that we do not sense the radical nature of the claim in the early days of the movement that Jesus was the Christ, the Messiah. In those early years, Christianity developed in relation to Jews where the title *Christ* carried a specific content. As it moved into and eventually became a largely Gentile religion, the issues raised by the claim that Jesus was Messiah became muted, and the title became part of a proper name.

Why was it such a radical claim? Both Jesus himself as well as His followers, at least after the Resurrection, interpreted His person and work in relation to the Old Testament Scriptures. Although Jesus himself avoided the messianic title throughout His ministry, almost immediately after He was resurrected His followers began making claims that He was the Fulfillment of the messianic hope (see Acts 2:22-36). Yet, loyal Jews who were well versed in the Scriptures had difficulty recognizing the validity of this claim. The reason was very simple: Jesus did not fulfill the Old Testament messianic hope in any literal sense.

This statement no doubt comes as quite a shock to

many who are accustomed to the popular method of speaking of the fulfillment of prophecy as evidence of the Christian faith. And even certain movements are formed to convert Jews to Christianity on the basis of prophecy. This approach has never been overwhelmingly convincing to those toward whom the efforts were directed, especially if they were informed about their faith and Scriptures. The record in the Book of Acts of Paul's preaching in the synagogues is evidence of this as he repeatedly turned to the more responsive Gentiles.

Contemporary Judaism still resists the Christian claim that Jesus of Nazareth is the Christ, and for the same reason. A report was carried in the September 17, 1993, issue of the *Nashville Banner* of a message given to a Rosh Hashanah service by Rabbi Stephen Fuchs decrying such evangelistic movements. His reasons for denying the Christian claim included first and foremost the fact that Jesus did not fulfill the messianic prophecies.

"Jesus met none of these Jewish requirements," Fuchs said. "He became the Messiah for those who became known as Christians because Christians altered the Jewish expectations and taught a new doctrine."

Of course, those who know their Bibles know this is partly true. It was not so much the Christians as Jesus himself who made this crucial transformation, and His followers came to see and appropriate it for their own self-identity. The "new doctrine" taught by Christians was that Jesus was the Messiah who suffered, a conception foreign to all Jewish thought. In the light of this, the words of Paul in 1 Cor. 15 take on a radical character as he recites the tradition he had received: "Christ died for our sins according to the Scriptures" (v. 3). No wonder he declared in 2 Cor. 5:16 the radical reorientation of his own thinking: "From now on, therefore, we regard no one from a human point of view; even though we once knew Christ from a human point of view, we know him no longer in that way" (NRSV). He had already spoken in 3:14-16 of the inability of the rabbi in the synagogue to understand his own Scripture until his heart (mind) turns to the Lord (Jesus).

Thus the claim that Jesus is the Christ involves a complete reinterpretation of the Old Testament and a reading of it in a nonliteral way. But in this claim lies the uniqueness of the Christian faith. Jesus indeed is the climax and culmination of God's redemptive action in the world. He entered our history, not to establish a political kingdom, as both the Old Testament and Jewish thought envisioned, but to establish the kingdom of God to rule first in the hearts of human persons and ultimately to be established throughout the earth.

A fuller understanding of this Christian claim may be had by examining the origin of the so-called messianic hope in the Old Testament. The term *Messiah* is not used in the Old Testament, but the hope is clearly present. It arose out of the reign of King David, whose rule captured the imagination of the Hebrew people. There were several characteristics that marked David's leadership. Two important ones were: (1) he defeated the Philistines, a well-armed military organization that had stood in the way of Israel's sole possession of the Promised Land for many years and had actually enslaved the people from time to time; and (2) he furthermore established a true kingdom for the first time.

Saul's kingship had been unsuccessful in accomplishing both of these, and he was little more than a tribal chieftain. These tremendous achievements by David, coupled with the promise of the Lord through Nathan that David's dynasty would have unending continuity, became the seedbed for the hope that there would someday emerge a king like David who would once again lead Israel to the glories that had marked the golden years of the Davidic era. Thus, every king who ascended the throne of Judah (the Northern Kingdom of Israel had no Davidic kings) was accompanied by the hope that he might be that kind of king, as certain coronation psalms indicate (see Pss. 2 and 110 as illustrations). These became known as Royal Psalms and thus part of the literature of the messianic hope.

Jesus as the *Christ* performed both those two major accomplishments as did David, but in a completely different arena. The enemy He defeated was not Rome or some other military or political power, but "demonic powers" (Col. 2:15, Barclay) under the dominion of Satan, who is "the prince of the powers of the air" (Eph. 2:2, ASV), and thus He potentially liberated all the children of Adam's race from the lordship of these enemies. As a consequence, He was able to establish a beachhead in human history that was interpreted by the Gospel writers as the inauguration of the kingdom of God.

His only Son. The title *Son* is likewise a title that came into full significance only after the Resurrection. It was then that the disciples came to recognize what Jesus had known all along: He had a unique relation to the Father.

As an Old Testament term, *son* was applied to Israel, to kings, and to any who enjoyed a relation of obedience to God. In other words, all who did the will of God could be described as "sons of God." In the early ministry of Jesus, especially as it is revealed in the Fourth Gospel, He carried out His work in explicit obedience to the Father's plan. While scholars debate the issue of Jesus' self-consciousness, it seems clear that He was fully aware, at least as early as the childhood Temple incident, that He enjoyed a special relation with

God. Consequently, we may say that Jesus did not become the Son of God because He was the perfectly obedient Servant, but He was the obedient Servant because He was the Son.

However, it is equally apparent in the Gospels that the followers of Jesus came to an awareness of this special relation with God because of their experience of His fully obedient life, living out a mission that was a continuing puzzle to them. This is the significance of the words of Paul in Rom. 1:4, where he speaks of Christ Jesus in His human descent but "who through the Spirit of holiness was declared with power to be the Son of God."

Our Lord. Lord, like the previous two titles mentioned in this paragraph, was also a post-Easter title so far as the followers of Jesus were concerned. It is actually the most exalted title of all and reflects the disciples' belief, to which the Resurrection had led them, that Jesus was God in the flesh. Peter's words in Acts 2:36 embody this faith.

Like certain other titles ascribed to Jesus, this one was used in the Greek world to refer to revered persons. It was sometimes an address of respect, like "sir." In 1 Cor. 8:5, Paul refers to the fact that there were "many 'lords,'" showing that the term was applied to numerous pagan deities.

However, when attributed to Jesus, *Lord* is taken from the Old Testament, where it is used to refer to the personal name of God himself. God revealed His name to Moses as Yahweh (Exod. 6:3), mistakenly taken over by later translators as Jehovah. In the course of time, this name came to be looked upon with such reverence that devout Hebrews were reluctant to have it on their lips. They used substitute words, one of the most prominent being the Hebrew word meaning "Lord."

Thus, when Jesus' followers called Him Lord, they

were identifying Him with the fullness of deity. The truth of this is seen by the fact that in the New Testament, passages in the Old Testament referring to God are used to speak of Jesus. For example, Phil. 2:10-11 is a quotation from Isa. 45:23, and Heb. 1:10-12 appropriates Ps. 102:25-27.

To call Jesus "Lord," which was probably the earliest Christian confession (and creed), was to grant to Him all the honor that belongs to God himself. This did not include the title "Father," however, but does lay the foundation for the later Christian creeds that affirmed that the Son was equal in nature to the Father.

By His resurrection, Jesus did not become "God" in some sense that He was not before. The Resurrection, however, was powerful proclamation of His deity, allowing those who believed to recognize clearly what they had only dimly grasped before—if at all.

The second section of this "article" of the creed makes two declarations about the earthly origin of Jesus: *Conceived by the Holy Spirit, born of the Virgin Mary.* These two phrases belong together, presenting two aspects of the same truth. If it were not for the second phrase, the first would only suggest the prevailing Jewish belief that every birth is accompanied by the activity of the Spirit of God. Each act of conception, as distinct from each sexual encounter, is the result of divine intervention.

Several rabbinic sayings embody this perspective. For example: "When husband and wife are worthy the glory of God is with them"; and "There are three partners in the production of any human being—the Holy One, blessed be He, the father, and the mother."[2]

The virgin birth of Jesus has become quite a stumbling block for the modern mind. Consequently, many have rejected it out of hand as being a legend or myth without foundation. Because of this rejection, some who hold to it as a fundamental of the faith have undertaken to vigorously defend it. They have chosen to make belief in it determinative of one's Christianity. Early in this century, a group of conservatives who came to be known as fundamentalists listed it as one of five fundamentals of the faith and often unchristianized any who disagreed with them.

Why does it create such problems? One of the major reasons is that it is contrary to the way normal births occur. The method modern historians use to establish the truth of claims made about events that occurred in the past is by paralleling them with contemporary events. If certain claimed events do not happen repeatedly according to the patterns of the normal flow of cause and effect, the conclusion is that such claims are fanciful. This means that unique events (one of a kind) are difficult to establish as true by the standard methods of historiography. But this same principle also makes it difficult to establish by scientific historical research the historicity of other events around which Christian faith clusters—for example, the Resurrection.

An extreme method of combating this difficulty is to appeal to the dictum of Tertullian in the second century, who said, "I believe because it is absurd." However, this church father was not speaking about the Virgin Birth, but about the Christian gospel of free forgiveness. There have been others who, oddly enough, have attempted to establish the validity of the Virgin Birth by appealing to the biological possibility of *parthenogenesis* (a biological term referring to reproduction by an unfertilized cell). Should this explanation be valid, it would accomplish the exact opposite of the intention of the miraculous birth. This makes such an argument especially dubious. In fact, preoccupation with the biological aspects of this belief really miss the essential truth involved, which is theological.

Most discussions of this theme in contemporary literature (aside from very conservative treatments) tend to emphasize the inconclusiveness of the evidence for a literal virgin birth. They point to the fact that only two of the four Gospels refer to it and that there is no further reference to it in the New Testament. Nowhere in Paul's writings is it presented as having any evidential value or is it used in establishing a theological position as is the Resurrection. Consequently, the attitude of these discussions is a "take it or leave it" attitude.

Many scholars draw the conclusion that since Mark and John make no reference to the Virgin Birth, they knew nothing about the "tradition." Far more likely is the thesis that their purpose was not furthered by telling this story, therefore they simply make no reference to it. One theory is that John 1:13 is a veiled reference to the Virgin Birth. Even though the argument from limited references carries no validity, we must grant the argument, however, that the New Testament does not explicitly make belief in the miraculous birth an essential element in salvation as it does belief in the Resurrection (see Rom. 10:9).

But it is not insignificant that very early in Christian tradition the Virgin Birth became a regular item in lists of Christian beliefs. Unless one chooses not to accept the authenticity of the accounts of Matthew and Luke, it would be difficult to "prove" the truth of this claim; but if one does acknowledge the integrity of the scriptural accounts, it then simply becomes a matter of seeking to identify the theological significance of this belief. Thus, we turn to that issue.

One proposal that has occasionally been made over the years can be rejected out of hand. This proposal rests on the faulty assumption that original sin is propagated from parent to child by means of the sexual act of conception. This rationale is flawed on two counts: (1) a physicalistic view of original sin and (2) a failure to take seriously the biblical doctrine of creation, which assures the goodness of all aspects of human existence. This does not mean that certain human drives cannot be perverted by human fallenness, but the body and its drives are not essentially evil. The idea would be that the only way Jesus could be born without sin would be through a birth that did not involve the transmission of sin. No serious biblical thinker could accept this view.

Interestingly enough, the phrase "born of the Virgin Mary" seems to have originally been intended to establish the full humanity of Jesus. We have already noted the presuppositions of the gnostics, who appear to be in the background of much of this creed. They would have no problem with accepting the divinity of Jesus, but real difficulty acknowledging that He was a flesh-and-blood person. Classical Christian faith insisted at every turn, however, that He was as fully a human person as any one of us, "sin apart."

Certain statements from the Early Church fathers, on the other hand, seem to use these phrases to refer to Jesus' heavenly origin. He was the Son of God because He was "conceived by the Holy Ghost." We have already surveyed the faith pilgrimage of the early followers of Jesus as they came to the recognition of His Sonship. However, by hindsight, they recognized that His Sonship did not begin with the Resurrection or at the baptism by John, but preceded all these stages in His ministry. He was the Son from the beginning. It must be added that to see His miraculous birth as validating His Sonship is not to suggest that it began at that point, since both the New Testament and subsequent Christian thought taught that He predated His birth into the human family.

Another theological significance that may be attached to the expression of belief that the Holy Spirit was especially active in the birth of Jesus stems from the belief that the Spirit is connected with the work of re-creation. For instance, in Ezekiel's vision of the valley of dry bones it was the Spirit of the Lord that energized the army of corpses assembled from the remains of Israel's former life. This life-giving power galvanized them into an effective force in the restoration of a new Israel (Ezek. 37).

At the time of Jesus' birth, there were numerous expressions of hope that once again God would bring about the deliverance of His people, even though the prospects looked dim because of the intimidating power of Rome. The activity of the Spirit in His birth was an indication that the deliverance was at hand, that the creative activity of God was again about to be released. What was not seen at first, however, was that the power to be broken was not political but demonic, and that the deliverance was spiritual in nature rather than nationalistic.

C. E. B. Cranfield, a leading contemporary New Testament scholar, suggests two additions to the theological significance of the Virgin Birth. One is to emphasize the discontinuity of the Incarnation with any purely natural causes. As he says, "Jesus Christ is not a savior arising out of the continuity of our human history, but God in person intervening in it, coming to the rescue."[3] This same emphasis is anticipated in a pictorial way in Isa. 53:2, in which the Suffering Servant is referred to as being like "a root out of a dry ground" (KJV). Dry ground normally does not produce growth. Jesus cannot be explained in terms of His culture, the Jewish religion, or the civilization into which He came. He can be explained only as from God.

A second suggestion of Cranfield is that the miraculous birth also attests to the fact that God's redemption of His creation is by grace alone. The "alone" in "grace alone" is here taken very seriously. "Our humanity, represented by Mary, here does nothing more than first accept—and even that acceptance is God's gracious gift."[4]

ᘒ PUTTING THIS CHAPTER TO WORK

Something Conceptual: Confirm or Refute Exercise

Refer to chapter 3 to *confirm* or *refute* each of the following statements:

1. The idea of Jesus being the *only* Son of God should be rejected by today's Christian. C ___ R ___ page ___
2. Contemporary Jewish religion resists the claim of Jesus' Messiahship on the basis that a suffering Messiah is a wrong idea. C ___ R ___ page ___
3. All Christian thought is an elaboration of the meaning of Jesus Christ. C ___ R ___ page ___
4. The most exalted title found in the Apostles' Creed is *Lord*. C ___ R ___ page ___
5. New Age attempts to "get in touch with yourself" are not in harmony with orthodox Christian religion. C ___ R ___ page ___
6. Jesus is the climax and culmination of God's redemptive action in the world. C ___ R ___ page ___
7. Very early in Christian tradition, the Virgin Birth became a regular item in lists of Christian beliefs. C ___ R ___ page ___

Something Devotional: Into the Word

1. Study Heb. 1:1-13; 4:14-16. List the descriptive

phrases and specific titles you find there for Jesus Christ.

2. Examine your own heart and life in prayerful contemplation of Jesus as

> *Lord*—in Max Lucado's words, this means that you make Jesus the Executive Director of your life.

> *Christ*—this refers to Jesus as the Anointed One, someone you should turn to, not turn off like a TV set.

> *Son*—not just a representative of God, but truly God.

Something to Do: Teaching Is Evangelism

Whether instructing our family, sharing in a prayer group, discipling a convert, or teaching a Sunday School class, most of us have teaching opportunities. Teaching can be evangelism. After all, the Great Commission is a command to go and "teach."

Whatever your next opportunity to teach about Christ, consider what you read or learned in chapter 3. Strategizing for the presentation, ask yourself these questions:

> What do I want them to understand?

> What do I want them to feel?

> What do I want them to do?

4

What Did Jesus Do?

The third paragraph of the second article of the creed focuses on the "work of Christ," sometimes referred to as the Atonement. But if we look at it this way, far more is included in His work than is envisioned in traditional theories of the Atonement. This may help us see the limited nature of the way we often think about the work of the Savior. All this may be summarized under the word *gospel*.

One of my delightful assignments is to serve on the Board of Ministerial Credentials of the district where I live. It often falls my lot to ask ordination candidates about their theological understanding. One question I have occasionally asked goes like this: "If I were a layman on a church board interviewing you as a prospective pastor, one of the most important things I would want to know is if you understand what the gospel is. Tell me—what is the gospel?"

I have received some interesting responses over the years, too often inadequate. This disturbs me. The correct answer is embodied here in this creed and is found primarily in the words *suffered under Pontius Pilate; was crucified, dead, and buried; the third day He rose again from the dead; He ascended into heaven, and sitteth at the right hand of God the Father Almighty; from thence He shall come to judge the quick and the dead.* To make it clear that there is a salvation dimension to these beliefs, the later Nicene Creed prefaces them with the words "Who for us men and for our salvation."

The word *gospel* is commonly defined as "good news." Some years back a member of the board asked me if I wouldn't just accept that for an answer. "Certainly not," I replied. When the nurse brought me the word that my wife had delivered a son and that both mother and son were doing well, that was good news, but it was not the gospel. No, the gospel is the good news that God, in the person of His Son, has invaded and acted in history one more time, and that event makes possible a salvation from sin.

Sometimes people want to include in the gospel a collection of abstract teachings or, even farther from the point, a group of ethical rules. But what we are seeing here is the biblical point of view at work. Look, for instance, at the confessions of faith in the Old Testament, such as Deut. 26:5-9:

> My father was a wandering Aramean, and he went down into Egypt with a few people and lived there and became a great nation, powerful and numerous. But the Egyptians mistreated us and made us suffer, putting us to hard labor. Then we cried out to the LORD, the God of our fathers, and the LORD heard our voice and saw our misery, toil and oppression. So the LORD brought us out of Egypt with a mighty hand and an outstretched arm, with great terror and with miraculous signs and wonders. He brought us to this place and gave us this land, a land flowing with milk and honey.

What you find here is the reciting of the story of God's activity in the history of the Hebrew people. The same thing is true with New Testament preaching such as we find in the Book of Acts. It too recites the history of the mighty acts of God but climaxes the story by speaking of God's last and greatest act as being His coming into human history in the person of His Son.

Note the words of Paul in 1 Cor. 15:1-4 as he summarizes the gospel:

> Now, brothers, I want to remind you of the gospel I preached to you, which you received and on which you have taken your stand. By this gospel you are saved, if you hold firmly to the word I preached to you. . . . For what I received I passed on to you as of first importance: that Christ died for our sins according to the Scriptures, that he was buried, that he was raised on the third day according to the Scriptures.

The words of the creed, like the words of the scripture, are lacking in flair. A few pointed words capture the essence of what it was all about. Really, there are two words that can provide the focal points for the total work of Christ: the word *suffered,* from the first phrase, and the word *judge,* from the last phrase.

These two terms point to the twofold character of the work of Christ. At His first coming He appeared as the Suffering Servant, who makes salvation available to all people through His death; at His second coming He will return to judge all men, based on the way they have responded to Him in His sacrificial self-giving.

These two events constitute the boundaries of the Christian era. And the time in between, in New Testament language, is called "the last days," the time between the times.

Swiss biblical scholar Oscar Cullmann has suggested a striking analogy to explain the significance and relation of these two happenings. He compares the first to D day—the time when the Allied forces landed on the

Normandy beaches and reestablished a foothold in Europe. From that time the outcome of World War II was never in doubt, although there remained a long mopping-up process. By this analogy we may say that in the Christ-event God established a beachhead in human history. In His death, Jesus took on in mortal combat and defeated the powers of evil. As a result of this decisive victory at the Cross, Satan's final loss in the struggle was guaranteed. No longer can it be said that Satan is "alive and well" on this planet—not if we take the New Testament seriously. However, D day awaited V-day, the time of the final consummation. In like manner, the triumph Jesus won at the Cross is to be demonstrated at His second advent. At His first coming His kingdom was inaugurated; at the Second Coming it will be consummated.

Jesus' return in glory as the Judge is one of the cardinal tenets of Christian doctrine. However, it is seen in the New Testament as the ultimate outcome of something that has already happened, not a visitation to accomplish a victory that the First Advent had failed to achieve.

Some time ago I developed a habit of greeting someone I knew with the question "What's the good word?" I quit doing this when an acquaintance quickly responded with the words "Jesus is coming again." I think he was a bit surprised when I remained silent. It suddenly occurred to me that the really good word is that Jesus has *already* come. And in His suffering and death He has assured the final establishment of His kingdom. His return will be to receive the scepter He has already won, which he received in the time of His humiliation.

But in addition to these two terminal events of the Christian era, there is also a reference in this last paragraph to an interim work. It is spoken of in terms of Je-

sus' session at the right hand of God, the Father. Thus
He is not an absentee conqueror but one whose conquest
has perpetual effectiveness in the life of the believer. We
now need to look at these three phases of Jesus' work in
more detail.

Suffered under Pontius Pilate. The historicity of this
event is established by tying it to the procurator of
Judea. Although Palestine was in an obscure corner of
the Roman world, it was part of a real world. These
events are not fanciful myths invented out of whole
cloth.

Influential theologian Karl Barth has highlighted
the importance of the historical character of these
events in the following dramatic words:

> This name in connection with the Passion of
> Christ makes it unmistakably clear that this Pas-
> sion of Jesus Christ, this unveiling of man's rebellion
> and of God's wrath, yet also of His mercy, did not
> take place in heaven or in some remote planet or
> even in some world of ideas; it took place in our
> time, in the centre of the world-history in which our
> human life is played out. So we must not escape
> from this life. . . . We are not left alone in this fright-
> ful world. Into this alien land God has come to us.[1]

Other than the Virgin Mary, Pilate is the only human being named in the creed, and he played an infa-
mous role in the passion of Jesus. Caught in a web of political intrigue, victimized by previous defeats in his
confrontation with the Jews, he found himself without
the moral fiber to do what he knew he should have done.

Barth further enlightens us by calling attention to
the fact, seldom noticed, that "the whole life of Jesus
comes under the heading 'suffered.'"[2] So often we limit
our vision of the redemptive work of Christ to the Cross

or the last week. There is good reason for this, since the Gospels themselves give so much attention to that last, climactic period of His ministry. But from beginning to end, if we will take notice, Jesus' life was marked by suffering, lightened only now and again by moments of joy.

Jesus experienced the suffering of rejection. Even as a child He was pursued with deadly intent, because His impending Kingship threatened Herod's exclusive lordship in the earthly realm where He lived. He suffered being misunderstood throughout the years of His public ministry, even by those who loved and followed Him. Even His family had serious questions about what He was about. In those intense hours leading up to His execution, He experienced the suffering of being ridiculed, He was abused and mistreated for no good reason except the delight of His captors, and finally He experienced the agony of being put to death by one of the most cruel methods known to men.

But He was God in the flesh. The implications of this truth were exceedingly difficult for early Christians to accept. They developed their theology under the influence of a Greek concept of God that removed Deity from the realm of time and space and made Him (or it) immune from suffering; He was, as they put it, "without passions." But "God was reconciling the world to himself in Christ," says Paul (2 Cor. 5:19), and one can only conclude that in doing so, God suffered.

But also this life of suffering manifested what sin is. To quote Barth again, "Sin means to reject the grace of God as such, which approaches us and is present to us."[3] John puts it this way: "He came unto his own [things], and his own [people] received him not" (John 1:11, KJV).

The key word here is *suffered* and must be recognized as being theologically quite different from the word commonly used in much of contemporary conservative literature. Under the influence of a theory of the divine-human relation based on legal concepts, it is often said that Jesus was *punished* for our sins. But this word carries a completely different meaning from the biblical understanding of how Jesus' work accomplishes our salvation.

The idea of punishment arises in the context of abstract law and finds its home in the lawcourt. When a crime has been committed, the criminal must be punished. When this legal mentality prevails, there is no possibility of forgiveness. Even if a surrogate is punished instead of the guilty party, the law remains intact, but no forgiveness occurs.

This is not the setting for reconciliation between God and sinful humanity. The suffering of God in Christ tells us that forgiveness occurs because God himself, in His Son, bears the suffering in His own person.

The pattern that provided direction for Jesus' ministry is found in Isaiah 40—55. There a figure appears, totally unanticipated by previous revelation. He is the "suffering servant of the Lord." The most familiar of five songs that speak of the servant is found in 52:13—53:12. Israel did not know what to do with this vision. Many feel it was the prophet's inspired vision of Israel's own destiny in the world as God's witnesses. But while she suffered—and has suffered since—from the Christian perspective it was Jesus Christ who lived out this vision in excruciating detail. The suffering of the servant was vicarious in nature, and the intent of it was to bear the sins of the world (see 53:6). Thus, to carry out God's redemptive purpose in the world, Jesus "suffered under Pontius Pilate."

Crucified, dead, and buried. The Jews had handed down the death sentence on Jesus, but they were legally incapable of carrying it out. Thus they came to their Roman overlords to do their dastardly work. The Romans often executed persons by the method of crucifixion, which was a slow and agonizing means of death, a symbol of degradation and ignominy. But Jesus' death by this method transformed the cross from a symbol of shame to one of glory, because it became the instrument by which He overcame the estrangement between humanity and God.

Oddly enough, however, the Crucifixion became a serious stumbling block to Jews and a challenge to Christians, to explain how a man dying on a cross could be God's Messiah. Had not Deut. 21:23 declared that anyone who died "on a tree" was under the curse of God? Thus early believers were hard put to explain how they could say of this "crucified criminal" that He was Jesus *the Christ.*

But the prophetic word had already anticipated this dilemma. It had said, "We esteemed Him stricken, smitten *by God,* and afflicted. But He was wounded for *our* transgressions, He was bruised for *our* iniquities; the chastisement for *our* peace was upon Him, and by His stripes *we* are healed" (Isa. 53:4-5, NKJV,[4] emphases added).

It seems strange to add the words *dead, and buried* to this clause. It is not simply because Paul did so in 1 Cor. 15:4, but rather for the same reason: to emphasize the reality of His death. At several points we have noticed the tendency of early believers under gnostic influence to reject the reality of Jesus' earthly, physical existence. This extended to the denial that His death really occurred, but was rather a mere charade. The repeated emphasis "dead and buried" was designed to deny this tendency.

Why was it important that Jesus be really dead? It

could easily have been the case that He might have survived the Crucifixion if He had been rescued quickly enough. The wounds need not have been fatal. In this method of execution, death was usually the result of exposure and complications resulting therefrom. An apparent death would have resulted in an "apparent" resurrection, and all would have been but an appearance.

At least one reason for stressing the reality of Jesus' death was the importance of His full identification with a sinful human race. As Paul says in 1 Cor. 15:22, the indisputable evidence that all are in sin is that "in Adam all die." Thus, if Jesus, as humanity's Representative before God, is going to effectively carry out this function, He must fully identify with humanity at the point of their deepest involvement in fallenness. Had He not truly died, was not really dead, this identification would have been incomplete, and His redemptive work flawed.

One does not bury a living person, but only one who has been deceased. Jesus was dead and they buried Him, and with Him they buried the hopes of all those who had pinned on Him their expectations for freedom. Disconsolate and defeated, they made their way back to their former life with only a memory to remind them of bright days that had seemed so promising.

Suddenly all that changed—because God raised this crucified, dead, and buried Person from the sealed tomb. But before we can celebrate the significance of this life-transforming event, we must take note of a mysterious phrase inserted in the creed at this point.

Descended into hell. This phrase was a late inclusion into the creed and has often been eliminated because of the difficulty of identifying its meaning. It has been the subject of much speculation. It seems to make no sense, especially if one takes the term "hell" as referring to the place of eternal separation from God.

One thing we can say for sure is that it does not imply that Jesus experienced the pains of this awful place. In some explanations of how His passion effected the salvation of mankind, it might seem consistent. In such views, Jesus became "the world's greatest sinner" because the sin of the world was attributed to Him, and as a sinner He experienced the consequences of sin in torment. There does seem to be a biblical text that supports this interpretation: as Paul says in 2 Cor. 5:21, "God made him who had no sin to be sin for us." But a possible interpretation is that He became a "sin offering" for us (see footnote in the NIV). This is how John Wesley translates it in his New Testament and so interprets it in his *Notes*.

The significance of this enigmatic phrase becomes quite plain when we realize that the Greek word here translated as "hell" is the word *Hades,* which simply means the place of the dead. Thus, it is simply another way of emphasizing the reality of His suffering and death, which He tasted for every person (Heb. 2:9). But the grave could not hold Him, and He came forth triumphant over death, hell, and the grave—the victorious Christ.

The third day He rose again from the dead. Anyone who understands the significance of the Resurrection recognizes that this is the most critical event in Christian history. Without the Resurrection, there would be no Christian faith. It is the linchpin that holds all intact.

In the old state capitol building in Frankfort, Ky., there is a beautiful set of stairs framed in a circular pattern. The two flights of steps extend from the first to the second level, moving in opposite directions from each other, then circling back to come together at the top. Each step interlocks with the one below and the one above—there is no mortar or other means of support holding them together. The whole is a unit, because at the pinnacle is a landing that locks into the top step on either side, creating a self-supporting staircase. If this stone landing were removed, the entire structure would collapse. So it is with the Resurrection. If it is not true, the structure of the Christian faith would collapse.

The Resurrection has four major implications. The first relates to the ministry of Jesus. We have already noted in looking at the title *Christ* that Jesus radically transformed the Old Testament concept. This was so different from the popular expectations that even His followers were constantly puzzled by what He was about.

Perhaps Jesus was mistaken! Perhaps He had misread the mission to which He was called! Perhaps He really was intended to establish a Jewish nationalistic kingdom with its capital in Jerusalem! Perhaps He should have mustered an army and overthrown Rome! Perhaps He really was not supposed to follow a path that led inevitably to rejection and death on a cross! If there was any doubt about this, the Resurrection dispelled it, because this return from the grave was God's validation of that mission. It was the Father's *"Good Housekeeping* Seal of Approval" on the way Jesus had transformed the Old Testament hope and carried out God's will.

No wonder the earliest Christian preachers saw themselves as witnesses to the Resurrection and saw this event as the elevation of this crucified Carpenter to the status of Lord and Christ (see Acts 2:36 and Rom. 1:4).

The Resurrection was furthermore the final blow in the defeat of Satan. In order to understand the significance of this statement, we have to review the prevailing understanding in Jewish theology at the time of Jesus' ministry. Long centuries of disappointment and frustration had eventually led many to give up hope that the promises made to Abraham and his descendants would ever be fulfilled within this age. They reluctantly concluded that God had withdrawn from history and could no longer be expected to intervene on their behalf as had occurred in past events, such as the Exodus. Using language that had been influenced by the surrounding culture, they came to talk about "this present age" (Titus 2:12), which was under the control of "demonic powers" (Col. 2:15, Barclay) with Satan as the "prince of the powers of the air" (Eph. 2:2, ASV). Hopes for the coming of the kingdom of God were thus postponed until "the age to come" (Heb. 6:5, ASV), which would be ushered in only when history had been brought to a halt. This, they believed, God would do through the destruction of existing society. This intervention would be accompanied by signs in the heavens, perhaps even "the earth" being "burned up" (2 Pet. 3:10, KJV) and replaced by "a new heaven and a new earth" (v. 13). In a word, they were pessimistic about "this present age."

The total ministry of Jesus had been pursued in the optimism that in Him the kingdom of God had entered history, even though "this present age" had not been brought to an end. Thus, those who believed in Him saw the work of Christ as a struggle with the powers that were in control. His miracles, especially those that involved casting out demons, were indications that "the age to come" had really invaded "this present age."

But the decisive struggle was at the Cross, and on the surface it appeared that Jesus had lost and the enemy had won. "On the third day," however, the true outcome of the battle was revealed, and it became apparent to all who believed that Jesus had indeed defeated Satan and his powers and demonstrated thereby that the kingdom of God was a present reality. Salvation did not have to wait until the end of the age but was available in the here and now. Sin does not have the last word, and Satan is a defeated foe. As Karl Barth so beautifully put it:

> The game is won, even though the player can still play a few further moves. Actually, he is already mated. The clock has run down, even though the pendulum still swings a few times this way and that. It is in this interim space that we are living: the old is past, behold it has all become new. The Easter message tells us that our enemies, sin, the curse and death, are beaten. Ultimately they can no longer start mischief. They still behave as though the game were not decided, the battle not fought; we must still reckon with them, but fundamentally we must cease to fear them anymore. If you have heard the Easter message, you can no longer run around with a tragic face and lead the humorless existence of a man who has no hope. One thing still holds, and this one thing is really serious, that Jesus is the Victory.[5]

In 1 Cor. 15, Paul identifies two more very important implications of the Resurrection. The first is found in verses 17-19: "And if Christ has not been raised, your faith is futile; you are still in your sins. Then those also who have fallen asleep in Christ are lost. If only for this life we have hope in Christ, we are to be pitied more than all men."

We have noted that in the work of Christ, biblical faith claims "the age to come" has already begun, although it has not yet been consummated. But one of the facets of the anticipated age to come as it developed in later Hebrew theological thought was that it would be the time of the resurrection of the dead. Thus, Jesus' resurrection was another indubitable evidence that the long-awaited day had arrived. His resurrection was not an isolated event, but rather it was the first moment in the final, general resurrection of the dead. This is what Paul means in 1 Cor. 15:20—"But Christ has indeed been raised from the dead, the firstfruits of those who have fallen asleep." When the question is asked, "When will the final resurrection occur?" the answer is "It has already begun."

Furthermore, in this context His resurrection is the guarantee of our resurrection. Throughout history is evidence that human beings have been searching for the answer to the secret of what lies beyond this life. Burial practices reflect a universal longing for immortality. Philosophers have attempted rational arguments to prove that there is an existence after death. Quasi-scientific practices have sought to provide evidence that there is "life after life." None of this is decisive. All attempts at proof still leave the human mind with the unanswered question of Job, "If a man dies, will he live again?" (14:14). Every experiment still leaves room for skepticism.

The strange Book of Ecclesiastes verifies this skepticism as it explores the limitation of experimental knowledge about the great human issues. It refers to this limited perspective as "under the sun." From this point of view, the possibility of determining if there is life beyond the grave is nil. As the author says in 3:19-21, "Man's fate is like that of the animals; the same fate awaits them both: As one dies, so dies the other. All have the same breath; man has no advantage over the animal. Everything is meaningless. All go to the same place; all come from dust, and to dust all return. Who knows if the spirit of man rises upward and if the spirit of the animal goes down into the earth?"

But in Jesus' resurrection from the dead, we have the one decisive evidence. As Paul says in 2 Tim. 1:10, "It has now been revealed through the appearing of our Savior, Christ Jesus, who has destroyed death and has brought life and immortality to light through the gospel." He really died! He was really buried! He was raised to a new order of existence, thus giving a foundation for a legitimate hope that, because He lives, we too shall live. The only possible skepticism here relates to the manner of this resurrected life, and we must leave that for the future, since it lies beyond our experience, and therefore we have no concepts with which we can describe it.

John Wesley's classical distinction between the fact and the manner can appropriately be applied here. We believe the fact, but we recognize that the manner is not revealed except in an analogy that still does not carry us into the realm beyond our experience. Consequently, as in other areas of mystery, we leave the manner to God and do not make it an object of faith. But we believe in the fact—because of the fact that "He lives."

Another present benefit hangs on the validity of Jesus' resurrection. Paul speaks of it in 1 Cor. 15:17—"And if Christ has not been raised, your faith is futile; you are still in your sins." This verse assumes the universality of sin by the word "still." The problem is how to gain salvation, to be delivered from this universal condition of alienation from God and corruption of nature.

There are only two logical ways for this to occur: we must either "bear our own sins," or God must bear them for us. The former is salvation by good works. But Paul everywhere shows the bankruptcy of this approach, and Christians throughout history who have attempted it have all had to throw up their hands in defeat and declare it to be impossible.

The reasons are numerous. For one thing, if one is

to be accepted by law keeping, the law must be kept perfectly with no exception, for if one is guilty of one misstep, the whole structure comes tumbling down. It is all or none. But even if it were possible to begin at this moment and flawlessly do all the law commands, what do we do about life before that? Everything we can do is all that is required. We have done that which is our duty to do. Thus, there is no way to make it retroactive by accumulating excess merit to cover earlier shortfalls. This, incidentally, highlights the weakness of thinking about salvation in terms of "merit," something the Western Christian Church has tended to do ever since the second century A.D.

But the real Achilles' heel of attempting to "bear our own sins" is the weakness of the flesh. As Paul says in Rom. 7:14, "We know that the law is spiritual; but I am unspiritual, sold as a slave to sin." "Flesh" here refers to the unregenerate human nature, not to the body, which is not sinful in itself. But our fallenness makes it a natural impossibility to so live that we can justify ourselves.

This leaves only one way, which is precisely the Christian claim. Jesus on the Cross is the empirical evidence that God is bearing the world's sin in His own suffering. But this is contrary to all merely human ideas. Man would say, "Salvation is by power and strength." The Scripture points us to Jesus and Him crucified (see 1 Cor. 1:18-25).

If Jesus—hanging in weakness and apparent defeat on the Cross, from all evidence under the curse of God—is truly God's Messiah and is thereby declaring that in love God takes our sin into His own heart, we need a guarantee that this is the case, since it goes contrary to everything we have come to believe through our human wisdom. And we have this guarantee in God's raising

Him from the dead. If there are only two ways to be saved—and one is bankrupt, while we have no evidence that the other is valid—it is as Paul said: We "are still in . . . our sins." But He is risen, and we may rest in the conviction that if we place our faith in the God who is in Christ reconciling the world unto himself, we are not in our sins any longer. This is why the apostle lays down the two prerequisites for being saved: to confess Jesus as Lord and to believe in our heart that God raised Him from the dead (see Rom. 10:9).

᪥ PUTTING THIS CHAPTER TO WORK

Something Conceptual: The Atonement— Questions and Answers

Answer these questions based on information in chapter 4.
1. What is the gospel?
2. What two words, according to chapter 4, provide the focal point of Christ's work?
3. What is the meaning of the phrase *the time between the times?*
4. Who is the only human being, other than the Virgin Mary, named in the Apostles' Creed?
5. What is the difference between *punishment* and the *suffering* that characterized the earthly life of Jesus Christ?
6. Why were the architects of the creed so careful to point out that Jesus was not only crucified but also dead and buried?
7. The creed says that Jesus "descended into hell [Hades]." Does that mean Jesus burned in the fiery torment of hell?

8. According to chapter 4, the resurrection of Jesus, by which Christianity stands or falls, has four major implications. Locate them in the chapter and list them in your journal. Reflect on their significance.

Something Devotional: **A Prayer to the Atoning Redeemer**

Use this prayer from the personal prayer journal of John Wesley in your daily devotions. Put a copy of it on the refrigerator, in your purse, in your Bible.

● Jesus, poor and abject, unknown and despised, have mercy upon me and let me not be ashamed to follow thee.

● Jesus, hated, calumniated, and persecuted, have mercy on me and let me not be afraid to come after thee.

● Jesus, betrayed and sold at a vile price, have mercy upon me and make me content to be as my Master.

● Jesus, blasphemed, accused, and wrongfully condemned, have mercy upon me and teach me to endure the contradiction of sinners.

● Jesus, clothed with a habit of reproach and shame, have mercy upon me and let me not seek my own glory.

● Jesus, insulted, mocked, and spit upon, have mercy upon me and let me run with patience the race set before me.

● Jesus, dragged to the pillar, scourged, and bathed in blood, have mercy upon me and let me not faint in the fiery trial.

● Jesus, crowned with thorns and hailed in derision;

● Jesus, burdened with our sins and the curses of the people;

● Jesus, affronted, outraged, buffeted, overwhelmed with injuries, griefs, and humiliations;

● Jesus, hanging on the accursed tree, bowing the head,

giving up the ghost, have mercy upon me and conform my whole soul to thy holy, humble, suffering Spirit.[6]

Something to Do: **Christlike Behavior**

When God chose to redeem the world, He chose to do so by giving himself in suffering service. He is our Pattern. We are to be echoes of His grace.

In which area(s) of your life do you most need a Christlike spirit of selfless giving?

1. In your social life
2. In your prayer life
3. At school
4. In relating to people of other races
5. In serving the church
6. In family relationships
7. On the job
8. In Bible study and serious reading
9. In the inner world of the imagination
10. In your generosity in giving
11. Other _____

What can you do today to so open your life to Christ that He can help you make progress in the areas checked above?

5

He Is Not Through Yet

He ascended into heaven, and sitteth on the right hand of God the Father Almighty. The completion of Jesus' earthly ministry did not end His redemptive work. His exaltation to the "right hand of God" inaugurates His rule from heaven in this "time between the times."

The means of this exaltation is embodied in the words *He ascended.* The Ascension is explicitly mentioned in only one passage, Acts 1:9: "After he said this, he was taken up before their very eyes, and a cloud hid him from their sight." The difficulty of understanding this in a literal sense in the context of our contemporary knowledge of the cosmos is apparent to any who will think about it. But the reality is probably to be found in the significance of the "cloud."

In Old Testament understanding, a cloud was indicative of the glory of God. The idea goes back to the cloud that guided the children of Israel through the desert (Exod. 13:21-22). The presence of God was particularly manifested by the cloud that hovered over the Tabernacle and became the occasion for worship (see 33:9-10). The cloud and the glory of God are synonymous. So as William Barclay says, "Any Jew and anyone who knew the Old Testament would see at once in the Ascension story, with the cloud into which Jesus was received, the reception of Jesus into the glory of God."[1]

Sitting at the right hand of a monarch signified administrative authority. We recall the self-serving ambitions of James and John, who desired this position of privilege under the false impression that Jesus' intentions were to establish a political kingdom. His response throws light on the meaning of His ascension as He asks them, "Can you drink the cup I drink or be baptized with the baptism I am baptized with?" (Mark 10:35-38). The way to exaltation was through servanthood and suffering. Now that He has passed through that experience, God is exalting Him to the position of preeminence as Governing Authority in the world.

John Calvin is cited as saying he did not find anything said about Jesus Christ being in a definite *place,* but about His having a definite *function,* namely, that of the exercise of divine power, comparable with that of a prime minister who, sitting at the right hand of his king, directs the government in the monarch's name.[2] This, then, is a metaphor telling us that even in the present the kingdom of God is the kingdom of Christ.

Exaltation to God's right hand is an additional element in the validation of His mission. It functioned in the same way as His resurrection. While we are not told explicitly, it seems reasonable that when Saul of Tarsus heard Stephen's dying words recorded in Acts 7:56— "Look . . . I see heaven open and the Son of Man standing at the right hand of God"—he was smitten with doubt about his own interpretation of the "pretender." That it clearly implied acknowledged deity to the Jewish hearers is suggested by their response: "At this they covered their ears and, yelling at the top of their voices [to drown out Stephen's voice] . . . dragged him out of the city and began to stone him" (vv. 57-58).

From thence He shall come to judge the quick and the dead. Marcion, the gnostic against whom this creed may have been written, or at least against similar teachings, taught that God is love. But misunderstanding the nature of the love that is God's nature, he denied any place for judgment. Thus, the creed affirms the truth of this aspect of the work of Jesus, in connection with His second advent.

There is no indication here, or in any other creed of the undivided Church, of anything other than a return in glory that will bring world history to consummation. The idea of a double coming, one for the Church and one for judgment, is totally foreign to both Scripture and creed.

Jesus himself spoke frequently of this return, as recorded in Matthew, Mark, and Luke. There are numerous references in which He referred to the coming of the "Son of Man" in judgment. What was so revolutionary was that He also used this title from Dan. 7:13-14 as referring to himself in His suffering. The One who suffers is the One who will judge.

The basis for the fact that both the "quick" (the living) and the dead will be included in the final event is found in 1 Thess. 4:13-18. These words offer encouragement to the Thessalonian believers that those who have "fallen asleep" will not lose their place in the kingdom of God when it arrives in fullness.

Many modern readers are put off by the language of the Second Advent. It is true that it is cast in terms of a cosmology to which we can no longer subscribe. To attempt to develop a visual picture of what will happen will simply look ludicrous, because we do not share the primitive worldview of a flat earth with a solid heaven like an inverted bowl above. Perhaps some persons do not sense the problem, but thinking people realize that we must acknowledge that the "how" of this hope may elude our comprehension. Nonetheless, along with the Church Universal, we look for the return of Christ to bring to completion the work He set in motion during His earthly ministry.

The same Jesus who "suffered under Pontius Pilate" will return to complete His work, and at that time the Kingdom He inaugurated at His first coming will be consummated. He came at the first advent as the Savior. He will come again as the Judge. How one fares at the coming in judgment will depend on how he has responded to the gift of salvation made available in Jesus' passion and resurrection. It takes both of these to complete the full purpose of God, which is the establishment of His kingdom among men.

The Christian confesses his belief that this final consummation will occur. If he takes the words of Jesus seriously, he will not waste his time attempting to determine *when* it will occur or even the order of events that will occur at the time. As respected theologian H. Orton Wiley said, "The events can never be untangled until prophecy passes into history, and we view them as standing out clearly in their historical relations."[3] This means that we cannot know in advance, but only after they have occurred, the shape and order of the last things. In a word, don't let your curiosity trap you into fruitless and unedifying speculations.

The question of judgment is also one that can create controversy as one tries to overliteralize the idea. Once again, to attempt to visualize a courtroom scene with God as Judge and uncounted multitudes of people standing to be evaluated will lead to mind-boggling results. But if we remember that the whole tenor of Scripture allows no hope for a second chance following our temporary existence, we must say that the Judgment is a way of telling us that we are responsible to God for our actions and that those actions have eternal consequences. Furthermore, the Judgment does not determine one's final destiny, because that has been settled by our response to God's overtures in our present probationary period. Rather, the Judgment will make obvious what has already been determined.

❧ PUTTING THIS CHAPTER TO WORK

Something Conceptual: Reviewing Ideas

1. One thing I had always heard about the second coming of Jesus that is challenged by chapter 5 is _____

_____

2. If I had to put the teachings of chapter 5 into one sentence, I would say _____

_____

_____

Something Devotional: A Song of Judgment

The *diamonte* is a poetic form that celebrates or explores the tension between opposites or seeming opposites. Often persons do not associate the judgment of God with "little Jesus, meek and mild."

In the diamonte, the opposites are placed at the top and bottom, only to be united in the middle line. Finish the diamonte that follows. Take careful note of the line numbers.

1. Noun
3. Two words that describe
   the word in line 1, *Jesus*
5. Three "-ing" action words
   that relate to the word in
   line 1, *Jesus*
7. A phrase that unites
   the top and bottom words:
   Jesus and *Judgment*
6. Three "-ing" action words
   that relate to the word in
   line 2, *Judgment*
4. Two words that describe the
   word in line 2, *Judgment*
2. A noun opposite or
   seemingly opposite the
   one in line 1, *Jesus*

1. ___*Jesus*___
3. ___*love mercy*___
5. _____ *forgiving* _____
7. _____
6. _____ *revealing* _____
4. ___*thorough justice*___
2. ___*Judgment*___

Something to Do: Judgment and Hope

Even as we greet the dawn, we know that night is only a handful of hours away. That certainty of nightfall casts a long shadow across our day. Judgment ahead— that's reality. But there's hope too. Charles Wesley put it this way in his well-known hymn "Christ the Lord Is Risen Today":

> *Love's redeeming work is done.*
> *Fought the fight, the battle won.*
> *Death in vain forbids Him rise.*
> *Christ has opened paradise.*

Or, as A. B. Simpson put it, as quoted in the March 23, 1977, issue of the *Alliance Witness* (p. 3), "Easter is the New Year's Day of the soul."

For family worship, a small-group meeting, or just for your own edification, prepare some posters or other items to display in your home that would remind your family or guests of the certainty of judgment, the hope of Christ's return, and the joy of eternal life. Would any of the foregoing quotations look good on your wall? How about this one from Fiona MacLeod? "At Easter . . . time bowed to eternity" (quoted in W. T. Purkiser, "The Rising of the Sun," *Herald of Holiness,* March 26, 1975, 19).

Three

THE HOLY SPIRIT OF CHRIST

The Holy Spirit is the living interiority of God.
—ROMANO GUARDINI

Before Christ sent the church into the world
He sent the Spirit into the church.
The same order must be observed today.
—JOHN R. W. STOTT

Those who have the gale of the Holy Spirit
go forward even in sleep.[1]
—BROTHER LAWRENCE

6

The Spirit, the Believer, and the Church

In the second article of the creed, we saw how the crucial historical facts of the Christ-event were affirmed as the gospel—the good news that is the basis of our salvation. Those events constitute the objective ground for our salvation. But if that is all there is, it is something that goes on outside of me and is a matter of slight interest. The New Testament also teaches that salvation is something that also happens *within* one (or within a community).

It is this inward element that is addressed in this third article of the creed and is the substance of the Christian confession about the Holy Spirit. To speak of the Spirit refers to God at work in the world, in me, and in the community of faith. It is the doctrinal way of saying that God is not afar off, but near at hand and applying the redemptive work of Christ to personal and communal experience.

While the creed does not attempt to speculate about the person of the Spirit but immediately addresses the issue of the saving results of His work, I want to suggest a truth that comes out in the structure of the creed. I am referring to the fact that the article on the Holy Spirit stands in the third position following articles on the Father and the Son. It is important that it stand in that position.

We may see the significance of this by referring to an ancient debate in the Church. It may sound rather musty, but I assure you—it is crucial to sound doctrinal understanding. The debate developed around the issue of whether the Holy Spirit proceeded from the Father only or from the Father *and* the Son. You could state it in a different way and ask, "Is the Spirit subordinate to the Father, or is He subordinate to both Father and Son?" You will immediately recognize that such an issue could not be settled by appealing to any Scripture texts. It could be determined only by theological considerations that attempt to capture the tenor of New Testament teachings.

The Western Church thinkers decided for the view that the Spirit proceeded from both Father and Son. I think they were right. The practical aspect of this is that the Spirit is clearly understood in the New Testament to be the Spirit of Christ so far as His character and activity are concerned. The Spirit of God came upon persons in the Old Testament period and endued them with power for service, even though some of these persons were not necessarily of the highest moral character. For example, consider Samson. But the New Testament gift of the Spirit is given to transform human character into Christlikeness.

I believe in the Holy Spirit. Let's note briefly here that we are using the title Holy *Spirit* rather than Holy *Ghost.* The latter was the name used in the original creed, and, believe it or not, there have been a few people who felt such a change in names indicated a kind of liberalism. But when the King James Version (1611) was translated, the word "ghost"—a derivation of the German *geist*—meant exactly the same thing as "spirit" in today's idiom. But it has taken on other connotations now. You can see how awkward it is when we try to say the "Ghost of Jesus" rather than the "Spirit of Jesus," which is a New Testament synonym for the Holy Spirit.

The holy catholic church, the communion of saints. It must first be clarified that the term "catholic" in this statement simply means universal. It has no specific reference to an institution. In the days of the creed, there was but one body of believers, and they were united in the Spirit.

It is significant that the first benefit mentioned as brought into being by the Spirit is "the church" or "the communion of saints." One would have thought that this would follow "the forgiveness of sins," but not so. Our contemporary mind thinks in different terms for two reasons. First, we think of the Church in terms of a denomination or organized institution, and second, we think about "being saved" and then joining the church. But this is quite contrary to the Bible. Theologically, the Church is prior to individual salvation. Not that it exists independently of individual believers, but such believers are constituted as the Church by the Holy Spirit. That means that to be saved is to be part of the Church.

This fact highlights the early Christian conviction that the essential nature of Christian experience is communal. The Church is not something you join after having become a Christian; becoming a Christian constitutes you as a part of the Church apart from which you cannot be saved. A careful reading of the early chapters of the Book of Acts will reveal that the Holy Spirit's outpouring was what created the community we see described on those pages. It is thus appropriate to refer to the Day of Pentecost as the birthday of the Church. Furthermore, most, if not all, of the instances recorded in Acts are of *groups*—rather than individuals—who experienced the indwelling of the Spirit. The old Israel had been constituted by circumcision and the law; the new Israel now is

constituted by the Spirit, without regard to social, economic, or ethnic considerations. "We are one in the bond
of love," and the "bond of love" is the Holy Spirit.

While it is true that the Church is a sociological
phenomenon subject to the laws of other social groups,
the difference is that the Holy Spirit transforms it into a
spiritual fellowship, a *koinonia*. Incidentally, this word
in Greek is feminine. It is something more than a volun-
tary association with one another; it is unity created by
participation in the divine reality of the Spirit.

One important implication of this is that the
Church cannot be formed by human hands. Denominational distinctives, organizational structures, charismat-
ic leaders, and so on can never of themselves guarantee
the Church. It is the work of God as He calls together
His people and creates community by His Spirit.

Another important consideration here that is more
implicit than explicit grows out of the connection of the
Holy Spirit with the historical Jesus, something we
have explored above. Just as Jesus was a real, bodily existence in contrast to a spiritual, nonphysical reality, so
the Church created by the Spirit is a visible congregation of real persons—not disembodied spirits. Many
Christian teachers today are questioning the traditional
distinction stemming from Augustine between the so-
called visible and invisible church. Karl Barth voices
this concern in these words: "It is best not to apply the
idea of invisibility to the church . . . In the Apostles'
Creed it is not an invisible structure which is intended
but a quite visible coming together which originates
with the 12 Apostles. The first congregation was a visible group, which caused a visible public uproar."[1]

This fact is both the glory of the Church and one of
its dangers. C. S. Lewis suggests in his classic book on
temptation that one way the devil can tempt young, ide-

alistic Christians is by calling their attention to the fact that the Church is composed of ordinary, perhaps even subordinary, people who have idiosyncracies and live quite ordinary lives in the world. The enemy's strategy, he suggests, is to get the idealist's attention on these things and never "let him see the church with its banners flying. This is to produce discouragement."[2]

Perhaps you have gone to church and looked over the congregation, listened to Brother A as he sang hymns off-key, listened to Sister B as she testified in butchered English, or watched the preacher struggle through a sermon he is trying to make heard over the screaming of a baby on the back pew whose mother doesn't seem to be aware that others are disturbed but nevertheless has no place to leave her child because the church is too small to afford a nursery—and asked yourself the question, "Is this what the church is all about?" If you have, you may need to follow C. S. Lewis's advice, demand that the enemy leave you alone, and ask God to help you to "see the church with its banners flying" so that with all Christendom you can say with conviction, "I believe in the communion of saints."

∽ PUTTING THIS CHAPTER TO WORK

Something Conceptual: I Believe

According to chapter 6, when a person repeats the Apostles' Creed, he or she affirms a pledge of faith that

1. The Holy Spirit is the Spirit of Christ as far as His character and activity are concerned.
2. The first benefit bestowed by the Spirit of Christ is the Church, the "communion of saints," a spiritual fellowship.

3. The Church cannot be formed by human hands—only the Spirit can create the Church.

Something Devotional: The Communion of Saints

The giant redwoods of California have stood tall against the howling storms for centuries now. You would think that with such an endurance record they would have roots that burrow deep into the mountainside and wrap themselves around huge boulders. You would think that—but you would be wrong. Actually, they have shallow roots.

How can they survive so long? They grow in groves, and the roots of many trees entwine. Thus they stand together against the storms as if to announce to the north wind, "We stand together. If you are going to take one of us out, you will have to take us all."

Sometimes a redwood does fall, almost always one that sprouted up some distance from the others. Its roots could not reach those of the other trees. Even a giant redwood cannot stand when it has to stand alone.

Christians are like that too.[3]

Ponder this and do whatever it takes to make this parable less disconcerting to you.

Something to Do: Five-fingered Prayer for the Church

For family worship, table grace, or a small group prayer meeting, plan and lead the following exercise in prayer.

1. The thumb is the strongest of the fingers. Pray for someone in the Church who is a powerful leader. Pray that the Holy Spirit of Christ will guide him or her.
2. The forefinger or first finger does most of the hand's

work. Pray now for some member of your family of faith who works, who perhaps has to work very hard. Pray that the Holy Spirit of Christ will give him or her strength. (Listen to the Spirit at this point. He may ask you to help the hard worker for whom you prayed.)

3. The middle finger is the tallest member of the "finger family." Let it represent someone in a high position. Pray that the Holy Spirit of Christ will give him or her humility and wisdom.

4. The next finger is the ring finger. Here one places jewelry like wedding rings, engagement or friendship rings, or class rings. These all speak of people who are precious to us. Pray now for someone very dear to you. Ask the Holy Spirit of Christ to bless and guide him or her.

5. Last comes the little finger. It is the smallest of all and the weakest. Pray for someone in your church who is small, powerless, poor, ignored, or weak right now due to unemployment or sickness. Pray to be the Spirit's servant in reaching out to such a person.

7

A Cure for Sin and the Gift of Life

The next phrase about the Spirit's work is *the forgiveness of sins*. While this affirmation is more a cause for rejoicing than a belief to be analyzed, if we analyze it we may find even greater cause for joy.

First, notice how the statement points to the Christian view of the human predicament. All sorts of theories have been advanced to explain the problem of humanity's dysfunctional existence.

Sigmund Freud, an extremely influential psychoanalyst, found the trouble in psychological maladjustment. The philosopher Karl Marx, father of Marxist communism, identifies it as the result of economic exploitation or in the structures of capitalist society. But the Christian diagnosis is that humanity's problem is sin.

What do we mean by this? The average churchgoer, if asked for a definition, would probably provide us with a list of things you do or don't do. That would not be altogether incorrect, but really, sin is much more profound than that. We need to distinguish between *sins* and *sin*. Sins, such as anger, greed, pride, and so on, are produced by a state of being that we call sin. By sin, Christian doctrine means our state of alienation from God, which in turn results in a situation of alienation from our brothers and sisters.

A simple illustration of what sin does to our human relationships is that of a symphony orchestra in which each instrumentalist takes his eyes off the conductor and begins performing on his own. The prophet depicted this truth so poignantly when, in Isa. 53:6, he said, "All we like sheep have gone astray; we have turned every one to *his own way*" (KJV, emphasis added). No wonder it is difficult for men to live in harmony.

The nature of this alienation has been variously called unbelief, pride, or egocentricity. In a word, it is declaring one's independence from God and becoming one's own god; a refusal to accept one's status as a servant and insisting instead on being the master.

Since our alienated state of being manifests itself in various ways, these manifestations are called sins—but while men forgive particular offenses against themselves, in relation to God, it is not so much the particular sin that is in view but the act of separation from God and the resistance to reunion with Him. One influential contemporary theologian has pointed out that the phrase "the forgiveness of sins" can be dangerous because it tends to direct the mind to particular sins and their moral quality rather than to the estrangement from God and its religious quality. However, when one has experienced the restoration of right relation with his Creator, it seems to me the sense of forgiveness of sins is a happy way to express that joy. No doubt that was what Horatio G. Spafford was sensing when he wrote these words of "It Is Well with My Soul":

> *My sin—O the bliss of this glorious tho't—*
> *My sin—not in part, but the whole—*
> *Is nailed to His cross, and I bear it no more!*
> *Praise the Lord, praise the Lord, O my soul!*

Forgiveness sounds easy! Many people take it lightly. The poet Heine was quoted as saying in his last hours, "Of course God will forgive me—after all, that's His business."[1] But it's not that easy. Forgiveness is a difficult matter, and Jesus' dying on the Cross is the eloquent testimony that in forgiveness God suffers.

Suppose someone very close to you, one whom you love deeply, betrays you and mistreats you miserably. Later on, that person asks you to forgive him or her. Do you think you could glibly say with a shrug, "Sure, I forgive—nothing to it"? I don't think so! The deeper the love, the more intimate the relation, the deeper the hurt and the more suffering is entailed in forgiveness.

And what about the One who loves us with an infinite love and is wounded deeply by our rejection? It is the truth of Jesus' death that God takes the suffering that accompanies forgiveness and bears it himself. It is in the forgiveness of sins that we experience the most profound expression of the divine love. Let us receive it with humble gratitude.

The resurrection of the body, and the life everlasting. These last phrases of the creed speak of "last things." This is what theologians call *eschatology,* a term that most readers have probably heard because there are fewer subjects that have received more attention in recent times, especially in the popular religious press. Books on this topic regularly stand among the top 10 in the best-seller list of religious books. This subject is such fertile ground for speculation, and people in such a precarious age as ours are so eager to hear some word about the future that it is easy to attract attention by announcing a topic relating to the end of the world.

However, the Apostles' Creed is quite reserved about this issue, as the biblically grounded Christian of today should be. Most denominational creeds in the Wesleyan tradition avoid making pronouncements that go beyond the clear teaching of Scripture. Instead they emphasize the relation of the final consummation to final salvation. The creed is a study in wisdom at that point.

The second article of the creed speaks of the central eschatological event, the Second Coming. It also speaks of one of the events that accompanies that occurrence and that relates to individual destiny: "the resurrection of the body."

If you look at the headlines of those flamboyant little "newspapers" displayed at the checkout counter of your local supermarket, you will sooner or later note a line saying something like, "Life beyond the grave proven." Maybe some of you remember the stir caused in recent years by a doctor's research about what he called "life after life." There is really nothing new about all this. Philosophers and theorists of all descriptions have from earliest times been probing at the door of death to attempt to establish some evidence of the immortality of the soul.

But note carefully that this is not what this Christian creed speaks about. It sees the destiny of the individual, not in terms of some disembodied existence, but in terms of the "bodily resurrection." It is the whole person who will inherit "the life everlasting." That this is much more contrary to natural human reason than the "immortality of the soul" is obvious from the fact that philosophers have repeatedly attempted to prove the latter on the basis of reason, but never the former.

In our earlier discussion of this creed we noted several times that much of it was directed against a false teaching known as gnosticism, which had as one of its basic beliefs the idea that the body was evil. If this were the case, then salvation would consist in escaping from the prison house of the body. But as we saw, the biblical view is that since God is the Creator, the body is good— and that furthermore man is incomplete without his body. Thus, the Christian hope of the life everlasting is grounded in the belief in the resurrection, and that hope is based upon the resurrection of Jesus Christ.

The Christian hope is not built upon rational argument, but upon the historical fact we explored in the second article of the Apostles' Creed. As Paul implies in 1 Cor. 15 in his argument to the Corinthians who appear to be denying the Resurrection, because He lives we shall live also. Although in this pivotal chapter he tried to provide his readers with an analogy of the seed falling into the ground, dying, and coming forth as a new form to help explain the resurrection body, I have to confess that it eludes my finite understanding. However, my faith is not in whatever I can fully understand, but in the power of God, who raised Jesus from the dead.

It is not a gloomy or morbid word, but an encouraging word to affirm in the graveside committal: "We . . . commit his (her) body to the grave in sure trust and certain hope of the resurrection of the dead and the life of the world to come, through our Lord Jesus Christ, who shall give to us new bodies like unto His glorious body."[2] With the saints of all the ages "I believe in . . . the resurrection of the body, and the life everlasting."

Jesus Christ is the Alpha and Omega, the first word and the last word. He spoke the originating word of creation (John 1:3) and will speak the final word of consummation. All Christian faith is a spelling out of the implications of who He was and what He did. From Him we know about the Father, and through Him we experience the gift of life through the Holy Spirit both here and hereafter. This is what the Apostles' Creed is all about.

✎ PUTTING THIS CHAPTER TO WORK

Something Conceptual: **Restating Truths**
Examine these quotes from chapter 7, and then re-

state them with pizzazz and punch à la "bumper sticker" style.

1. "By [the state of] sin, Christian doctrine means our state of alienation from God, which in turn results in a situation of alienation from our brothers and sisters."

2. "The nature of this alienation [sin] has been variously called unbelief, pride, or egocentricity."

3. "One . . . theologian has pointed out that the phrase 'the forgiveness of sins' can be dangerous because it tends to direct the mind to particular sins and their moral quality rather than to the estrangement from God and its religious quality."

4. "In the forgiveness of sins . . . we experience the most profound expression of the divine love."

5. "It is the whole person who will inherit 'the life everlasting.'"

6. "My faith is not in whatever I can fully understand, but in the power of God, who raised Jesus from the dead."

Something Devotional: The Apostles' Creed

1. Prayerfully recite the Apostles' Creed. Surely you know it by now. Repeat it, not to prove you know it by heart, but to let its every phrase sink into your heart.

2. Prayerfully sing the Gloria Patri.

3. Read again the words of Laurie Du Bose at the beginning of part 1 of this book.

Something to Do: Spread the Word

1. Write a letter to your pastor, explaining why you think it is a good idea to use the Apostles' Creed often in public worship.

2. Send a similar letter to the Worship Committee or its equivalent in your church.

3. Buy a copy of this book for someone who could use it. (OK, so you can't afford to buy an extra copy—at least *loan* this book, but be sure to tell the person you want it back.)

NOTES

Preface

1. James B. Chapman, *A Christian: What It Means to Be One,* rev. ed. (Kansas City: Beacon Hill Press of Kansas City, 1967).
2. Ibid., 11.
3. H. Orton Wiley, *Christian Theology,* 3 vols. (Kansas City: Beacon Hill Press, 1940-43), 1 (1940): 42.

Part One

1. Laurie H. Du Bose "'Tis Then," *Alliance Life* (formerly *Alliance Witness*), June 6, 1984, 2. Used by permission. *Alliance Life* is the official magazine of the Christian and Missionary Alliance.

Chapter 1

1. Alan Richardson, *Creeds in the Making* (Philadelphia: Fortress Press, 1981), 8.
2. J. N. D. Kelly, *Early Christian Creeds* (New York: David McKay Co., copyright by Longman Group Ltd., 1972), 1-2.
3. Ibid., 100-104.
4. Stated in a sermon preached on the National Radio Pulpit, date unknown.
5. See David H. C. Read, *The Christian Faith* (New York: Walker and Co., 1985; originally published by Abingdon Press, 1956), 157-58.

Chapter 2

1. For an excellent discussion of these issues, as well as one of the most usable proposals for addressing the problem, see John Bright, *The Authority of the Old Testament* (Grand Rapids: Baker Book House, 1975).
2. G. Ernest Wright and Reginald H. Fuller, *The Book of the Acts of God* (Garden City, N.Y.: Doubleday and Co., 1957), 109.
3. Karl Barth, *Dogmatics in Outline* (London: SCM Press, 1960), 49.
4. William Temple, *Nature, Man, and God* (London: Macmillan and Co., 1935), 478.

Part Two

1. Robert Browning, quoted in *Religion in Life,* Autumn 1978, 353. Title of poem is not provided by source.
2. Carroll E. Simcox, comp., *3,000 Quotations on Christian Themes* (Grand Rapids: Baker Book House, 1988), 135.

Chapter 3

1. The first listing of the documents in the New Testament canon as we

have them today appeared in A.D. 367 in the Easter Letter of Athanasius. See Alex R. G. Deasley, "Canon," in *Beacon Dictionary of Theology*, ed. Richard S. Taylor, J. Kenneth Grider, and Willard H. Taylor (Kansas City: Beacon Hill Press of Kansas City, 1983), 90.

2. Quoted in William Barclay, *The Apostles' Creed for Everyman* (New York: Harper and Row Publishers, 1967), 84.

3. C. E. B. Cranfield, "Some Reflections on the Subject of the Virgin Birth," *Scottish Journal of Theology* 41 (1988): 2, 189.

4. Ibid.

Chapter 4

1. Barth, *Dogmatics in Outline,* 109.

2. Ibid., 102.

3. Ibid., 105.

4. The *New International Version* uses the term "punishment" (for "chastisement"), which is an incorrect rendering and reflects the Calvinistic theology of the translators.

5. Barth, *Dogmatics in Outline,* 123.

6. Donald E. Demaray, ed., *Devotions and Prayers of John Wesley* (Grand Rapids: Baker Book House, 1957), 36-37.

Chapter 5

1. Barclay, *Apostles' Creed for Everyman,* 171.

2. Cited in Karl Barth, *Credo* (New York: Charles Scribner's Sons, 1962), 106.

3. Wiley, *Christian Theology* 3 (1943): 307.

Part Three

1. The three quotations on this page are printed without further reference in *3,000 Quotations on Christian Themes,* Carroll E. Simcox, comp. (Grand Rapids: Baker Book House, 1988), 19, 20, 21 respectively.

Chapter 6

1. Barth, *Dogmatics in Outline,* 142.

2. C. S. Lewis, *The Screwtape Letters* (New York: Macmillan Publishing Co., 1961), 12-13.

3. Wesley D. Tracy et al., *The Upward Call: Spiritual Formation and the Holy Life* (Kansas City: Beacon Hill Press of Kansas City, 1994), 135. Used with permission. All rights reserved.

Chapter 7

1. Quoted in Donald M. Baillie, *God Was in Christ* (London: Faber and Faber, 1961), 172.

2. *Manual of the Church of the Nazarene, 1993-97* (Kansas City: Nazarene Publishing House, 1993), 251.

OTHER SELECTED BOOKS ON THE APOSTLES' CREED

Barclay, William. *The Apostles' Creed for Everyman.* New York: Harper and Row Publishers, 1967.

Barr, O. Sydney. *From the Apostles' Faith to the Apostles' Creed.* New York: Oxford University Press, 1964.

Barth, Karl. *Credo.* New York: Charles Scribner's Sons, 1962.

———. *Dogmatics in Outline.* London: SCM Press, 1960.

Kelly, J. N. D. *Early Christian Creeds.* New York: David McKay Co., copyright by Longman Group Ltd., 1972.

McGiffert, Arthur Cushman. *The Apostles' Creed.* New York: Charles Scribner's Sons, 1902.

Pannenberg, Wolfhart. *The Apostles' Creed.* Philadelphia: Westminster Press, 1972.

Thielicke, Helmut. *I Believe.* Trans. John W. Doberstein and H. George Anderson. Philadelphia: Fortress Press, 1968.

OTHER
BEACON HILL BOOKS
BY H. RAY DUNNING

**Biblical Resources
for Holiness Preaching**
(2 Volumes)
083-411-5085

**Grace, Faith, and Holiness:
A Wesleyan Systematic Theology**
083-411-2191

Introduction to Wesleyan Theology
(coauthored with William M. Greathouse)
083-411-1349

A Layman's Guide to Sanctification
083-411-3872

**The Second Coming:
A Wesleyan Approach
to the Doctrine of Last Things**
083-411-5255

*Purchase from your favorite bookstore,
or order directly from*

Beacon Hill Press of Kansas City
Kansas City, Missouri
1-800-877-0700